ART AND HISTORY OF
TEL AVIV YAFFO

BONECHI & STEIMATZKY

Aerial view of Tel Aviv.

INDEX

Historical Outline ....*Page 3*

TEL AVIV 5

-Bialik House 15

-Bialik Square 15

-Bird Safari 46

-Central Library 35

-City Hall 36

-The City on the sea 47

-Diamond Exchange 44

-Diaspora Museum..41

-Dizengoff 5

-Dizengoff Square 6

-Dizengoff Street 9

-Edith Wolfson Park 44

-Ha'aretz Museum 39

-Habimah Theater 9

-Helena Rubinstein Pavilion 10

-Kikar Hamedina..36

-Mann Auditorium 9

-The Modern City 19

-New City Hall 35

-Rubin Museum 12

-Shuk Hacarmel 16

-Tel Aviv Museum of Art................................22

-University 41

YAFFO (Jaffa) 56

Historical Outline

The imposing urban nucleus of Tel Aviv - Jaffa lies in a marvelous position overlooking the Mediterranean. This impressive and spectacular metropolis, situated near the estuary of the Yarkon River, south of the farflung plain of Sharon, extends along the coast for almost eight kms., and moves back into the hinterland for about four. Tel Aviv, with its 328,000 inhabitants, is the administrative seat of the Tel Aviv District (66 sq. miles/170 sq. km.) which numbers a population of over a million. Greater Tel Aviv thus can be considered one of the outstanding metropolises in the Middle East and in Israel is second in importance only to Jerusalem. Anyone under the impression that monumental ruins or vestiges of the past are to be found in Tel Aviv will probably be in for disappointment. Practically all that bears witness to past history are a few tombs, dating to the Middle Bronze Age, unearthed in Tel Quasile, and the ancient remains of fortifications, which came to light near the course of theYarkon River. It must constantly be kept in mind that, unlike many other cities in Israel and in this part of the East in general, Tel Aviv is really too young and modern to have much in the way of history and is a direct offshoot of Jaffa, the oldest harbor in the world. In Hebrew "Tel" means artificial mound, composed of the remains of ancient settlements that were abandoned, while "Aviv" is to be interpreted as "spring" or as "life which renews itself". In 1909 Tel Aviv, the "Hill of Spring", came into being in the desert landscape of the dunes which lined the coast near the estuary of the Yarkon River. It was originally a small residential suburb, almost a garden city, created by a group of Jewish families who resided and worked in the Arab center of Jaffa. The small settlement rapidly increased in size, a focal point for the Jewish people, and soon outgrew its mother city. The forcible evacuation of Tel Aviv and Jaffa by the Turks during World War I put a halt to this incontrollable growth but it immediately started up again after the Balfour Declaration (Nov. 2, 1917), regarding the establishment of a Jewish State in Palestine. In 1922 Tel Aviv obtained the "status" of city, although it remained under the administration of Jaffa, while the following year the new autonomous administration began to take shape. The years preceding World War II marked still further growth in population, with the arrival of masses of Jewish refugees fleeing from Nazi persecution. On May 14, 1948, David Ben Gurion proclaimed the creation of the State of Israel in Tel Aviv, and became Prime Minister. Tel Aviv was the first Jewish only town, founded when Palestine had many cities with mixed Jewish/Arab population and there were regular unrests. In 1950 administrative unification with Jaffa was achieved. Tel Aviv nowadays is the principal center of Jewish tourism, a city throbbing with life, the cultural pole and the economic hub of entrepreneurial activity, finance, industry (chemical, publishing, graphics, mechanics, textile, the processing of tobacco and wood, cement factories), and is the very image of a highly efficient and functional modern city. Its skyline of high rise buildings and towers, its night life and countless meeting places for tourists and the good-looking Israeli youth, mirrors the modern State of Israel. While it may be true, as someone wrote, that the city lacks the dignified solemnity of Jerusalem, and the mysterious murmurs of Haifa (see Malka), the old folk adage fits to a T - "in Tel Aviv one lives one's life, in Jerusalem one prays and in Haifa one works."

4

Tel Aviv, two views of Dizengoff Center dominated by the skyscrapers.

TEL AVIV

DIZENGOFF

The city center

Although called a quarter, basically Dizengoff is simply the pulsating nucleus and motor force of life in the city. Centrally situated, the area includes Dizengoff Square (*Kikar Dizengoff*), on which the important city streets converge, and the large thoroughfare of the same name. Dizengoff Street is noted for the high rise buildings which line it, for the particular atmosphere, for its modern commercial and business complexes with *Dizengoff Center* in the lead, and for the picturesque rows of cafès which line the sidewalks in a variegated pattern of tables and chairs, inviting the tourist, and the citizen as well, to stop and take a break. Shop windows, elegant boutiques, but above all cafés and restaurants, stand one after the other in cheerful array along *Dizengoff Street*. Some of these were tradi-

tional points of encounter for men of letters and the intelligentsia. And still are. Cafés such as the *Rowal* and the *Kassit* were once well known and some like the *Café Afarsemon* and the *Batya* are still particularly popular. On weekends especially, friends and the gilded youth of Tel Aviv, out for a good time, crowd around the tables of the *Café Cherry*.
This street of Tel Aviv is a bit Via Veneto, Fifth Avenue and the Paris boulevards all in one, furnishing the regular customers with the chance to contemplate a sea of humanity composed of idlers, business men, tourists, famous actors or singers, well-known and lesser-known personalities, all drawn together in the collective rite of the joy of living and of becoming part of the frenetic and holiday atmosphere of Tel Aviv by night.

Tel Aviv, Dizengoff Center, the shopping center,
exterior and interior.

Tel Aviv, the striking Fountain of Fire and Water, by
Yaacov Agam, in Dizengoff Square.

Tel Aviv, a picture of Dizengoff Square.

DIZENGOFF SQUARE

Dizengoff Square (*Kikar Dizengoff*) with its palms
and modern *Fountain of Fire and Water* represents
the essence of the futuristic urban concept of this
great city of the Middle East. The intense car traffic
flows below the pedestrian area which is one of the
most popular rendevouz sites in Tel Aviv.

The square is named after Zina Dizengoff, wife of
Meir Dizengoff, first mayor of Tel Aviv, elected in
1920, who played such an important role in provid-
ing his city with an efficient administrative autono-
my.

The ultramodern **Fountain of Fire and Water**, a
work by Yaacov Agam, is exceptionally striking. It
is in aluminum and steel and particularly at night
diffuses beams of colored light and luminous sceno-
graphic effects.

Tel Aviv, some of the elegant shops on Dizengoff Street; a view of the Mann Auditorium overlooking the square and two views of the Habimah Theater.

DIZENGOFF STREET

As mentioned previously, this street is one of the main axes of the city center. Of particular note among the numerous business activities is the *Steimatzky Bookshop*, the oldest and most famous in the entire country. For those who love to go shopping, the **Dizengoff Center**, a modern and functional shopping center installed on several floors, is a must.

MANN AUDITORIUM

Modern in concept, the auditorium is named after *Frederic Mann*. The main facade faces out on a square full of palms, gardens and a pool with waterworks. Acoustics are excellent and it has an audience capacity of up to 3,000. The *Israeli Philharmonic Orchestra* performs its concerts here.

HABIMAH THEATER

This futuristic construction, fronted by a curious abstract sculpture, dominates the square of the same name and is where the performances of the *National Jewish Theater*, begun by Russian Jews who came here in the late 1920s, are given. The theater was founded in 1945 and was radically renovated in 1970.

9

HELENA RUBINSTEIN PAVILION

Dizengoff Street is also the cultural center of the city: the Helena Rubinstein Museum of Modern Art is housed in the modern pavilion on the corner of *Tarsat Street*. Permanent and temporary exhibitions of modern art, in particular of works of Jewish artists throughout the world, are held in this building, situated close to the Mann Auditorium.

Tel Aviv, two views of the Helena Rubinstein Museum of Modern Art.

Tel Aviv, entrance to the Rubin Museum and one of its rooms.

Rubin Museum: Girl with Dove (1929).

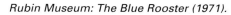

Rubin Museum: The Engaged Couple (1929).

Rubin Museum: The Blue Rooster (1971).

Rubin Museum: The Old City (1925).

Rubin Museum: The Harbor of Jaffa (1922).

RUBIN MUSEUM

Reuven Rubin, perhaps Israel's most famous painter, was born in 1893 in Galatz, Rumania, and died in Tel Aviv on October 13, 1974. It was the artist's wish to have his private home turned into a museum, and the result is the Rubin Museum which is open to the public thanks also to the contribution of the City of Tel Aviv. Rubin left the Museum 45 canvases which document his artistic career. Some of these are part of the Museum's permanent collection on the ground floor.

The first floor houses a biographical exhibition of the artist's life, with documents and photographs, a room with exhibitions of graphic art, a library and a reading room open to the public.

The painter's studio has been faithfully reconstructed on the second floor.

Rubin was closely bound to the land of Israel, the land where he found himself and which witnessed the flourishing of his extraordinary talent. His paintings show us the land as he saw it in all its fullness: mountains and cities, gardens and valleys, old people and women, Jews and Arabs, plants and stones, all set together to create surprising combinations on a small piece of canvas.

13

Tel Aviv, Bialik Square: the Old Town Hall and the Monument facing the square, as well as a detail of the mosaic decoration.

Tel Aviv, exterior of the Bialik House and one of its rooms.

BIALIK SQUARE

A rather singular **monument**, decorated with lively mosaics which illustrate the *Development of the City*, stands at the center of this small square. At one side is the old **town hall**, initially planned as a hotel but never realized (1925), which now houses the **Historical Museum of Tel Aviv and Jaffa**.

BIALIK HOUSE

This typical house, which in concept draws on Mediterranean and in particular Levantine architecture, was built in the mid-1920s. Chaim Nahman Bialik, Israeli's national poet, lived here. Inside is a small museum, with manuscripts and memorabilia.

SHUK HACARMEL

The Carmel Market is set in the heart of the Yemenite quarter. It is well worthwhile visiting this typically oriental part of the large city. The picturesque confusion of stands, exotic perfumes, brilliant hues mingled with the cries of venders furnishes an idea of the authentic folk traditions and local color of the Israeli metropolis.

Tel Aviv, Shuk Hacarmel: these picures give you an idea of the picturesque atmosphere and the variety of merchandise offered at the Carmel Market, in the Yemenite quarter.

THE MODERN CITY

While Tel Aviv may basically be a 'young' city, no more than a few decades old, certain aspects of its architecture and structure make it a metropolis which can vie in skyline with the best known cities in Europe or around the world.

Take the **Shalom Tower (Peace Tower)**, for instance, with its silhouette which rises high above the low houses of the southern part of Tel Aviv. Its 140 meters (37 floors) make it one of the tallest buildings in the Middle East. It was begun at the end of the 1950s when some of the preexisting urban fabric was torn down, including the prestigious school, the *Herzliya Gymnasium* (1909). The tower, which contains shops, warehouses, offices, a bank and the interesting **Wax Museum**, has a panoramic terrace. From the top, haze permitting, it is possible to see Haifa's Mount Carmel, Jerusalem and the Negev Desert.

Tel Aviv, two pictures of the Shalom Tower with the War Memorial.

Tel Aviv, Rothschild Boulevard (Sderot Rothschild), and the War Memorial.

Tel Aviv, the Rothschild Building and a detail.

Among the other 'vertical' elements of Tel Aviv, note should be taken of the **Rothschild Building**, an evocative and futuristic skyscraper sheathed in glass.

The daring silhouette of the **Telecommunications Tower** dominates the building beneath. Various pieces of modern sculpture by Henry Moore have been set in the square in front of this complex.

In the vicinity of the **Asia House**, with its unique architectural design which calls to mind the sinuous outlines and the force of the waves of the sea, is the **IBM Building**, a skyscraper which is the pride of modern Israeli architectural concepts. Particular note should be taken of the base, curiously tapered and fluted with respect to the cylindrical body of the skyscraper itself.

America House, an architecturally avant-garde complex of buildings, is also part of this town planning context.

The first neighborhood of Tel Aviv was *Newe Tsedek* and now houses the **Susan Dalal Center** for performing arts.

Tel Aviv, the modern Telecommunications Tower looms up behind a sculpture by Henry Moore.

Tel Aviv, view of the Court House and the IBM Building.

Tel Aviv Museum of Art: the facade. In the foreground: "Reclining Figure", bronze sculpture by Henry Moore, 1969-70.

Roy Lichtenstein: Tel Aviv Museum Mural, 1989. Oil-based Acrylic (Magna) on canvas.

Yaacov Agam: Pace of Time, 1970. Aluminium.

TEL AVIV MUSEUM OF ART

The Tel Aviv Museum was established in the home of the first Mayor of Tel Aviv, Meir Dizengoff. Works of art which constituted the base of the Museum's Collection were displayed, including works by international Jewish artists, mainly from the Paris School such as Chagall -who was actively involved in the founding of the Museum- Mane Katz, Uri Lesser and Modigliani.

Alongside these, works by Israeli artists -Reuven Rubin, Nahum Guttman, Joseph Zaritzky, Arie Lubin and Anna Ticho -were shown.

In the thirties the first concerts were held at the Museum and it became a cultural center for the city of Tel Aviv. In 1959, after Dizengoff's home had become too small, the Museum's Helena Rubinstein Pavilion for Contemporary Art exhibitions was inaugurated, and in 1971 the Museum opened its beautiful, large new building on Shaul Hamelech Blvd. In 1993 with the growth of the Museum's collections, further renovations were completed and another 8,000 square meters of exhibition space was added. In addition to the exhibition halls, the Museum also houses the Helena Rubinstein Art Library, the Graphics Study Room, a cafeteria and a shop. In 1987 the Museum's Art Education Center was established and workshop for children, youth and adults are held in the plastic arts, video, photography, theatre, etc. Today the Tel Aviv Museum of Art welcomes over 400,000 visitors annually and serves as a cultural center for the greater Tel Aviv metropolitan area. Events at the Museum include concerts, lectures, recitals, music, cinema and special events in the Recanati Auditorium (seats 520) and the Kaufmann-Gitter Hall (seats 200).

23

Tel Aviv Museum of Art. Peter Paul Rubens:
Portrait of Madame de Vicq, 1625.

Tel Aviv Museum of Art. Maurycy Gottlieb:
Jews Praying in the Synagogue on Yom Kippur, 1878.

Tel Aviv Museum of Art. Jan Brueghel the Younger and
Hendrick van Balen: An Allegory of the Four Elements,
c. 1630.

*Tel Aviv Museum of Art. Auguste Renoir:
Nude seen from the Back, 1876.*

*Tel Aviv Museum of Art. Paul Signac:
Pont Mirabeau, 1903.*

Tel Aviv Museum of Art. Vincent van Gogh:
The Shepherdess, after Millet, 1889.

Tel Aviv Museum of Art. Pablo Picasso:
Mother and Child by the Sea, 1901.

Tel Aviv Museum of Art. Yitzhak Danziger:
Sheep in the Negev, 1951-1969.

Tel Aviv Museum of Art.
Igael Tumarkin:
Butchers, 1968-69.

Tel Aviv Museum of Art.
Yoseph Zaritzky: Yehiam II, 1961.
Diptich.

Tel Aviv Museum of Art. Avigdor Stematzky:
Heart inspired Pictures, 1982.

Tel Aviv Museum of Art. Gustav Klimt:
Friedricke Maria Beer, 1916.

Tel Aviv Museum of Art. Yehezkel Streichman:
Ein Hod, 1956.

Tel Aviv. These pictures document the daring engineering of the IBM Building and the unique architectural solution of the base.

On pages 32 and 33: pictures of the curious silhouette of Asia House, with the IBM Building rising up above it, and some modern buildings around America House.

CENTRAL LIBRARY

This important cultural institution, the **Shaarey Zion Library**, is housed in a building that is quite in keeping with the advanced architectural concepts that characterize Tel Aviv.

It was founded in the last decade of the 19th century. Today over 100,000 volumes in various languages are available for consultation in its pleasant study and research premises.

NEW CITY HALL

The *Ibn Gvirol* (a broad boulevard in the northen part of Tel Aviv) runs along one side of the New City Hall which overlooks the spacious Kings of Israel Square (*Kikar Malkhei Yisra'el*), with its flowerbeds and trees and palms. Various fairs take place in the square throughout the year, first and foremost the annual Book Fair. The City Hall building, with City Hall skyscraper rising up behind it, is a modern twelve-floor structure with a panoramic terrace.

Tel Aviv,the New Town Hall overlooking Kings of Israel Square.

Tel Aviv, a view from on high of Kings of Israel Square, particularly animated on the occasion of the annual Book Fair, with the New Town Hall and the skyscraper of the 'City Hall' complex in the background; a boulevard flanked by palms across from Kings of Israel Square.

CITY HALL

This shopping center which takes its name from the nearby Town Hall, is one of the best of its kind in this great urban center of the Middle East. Modern exhibition infrastructures house the various shops with their elegant refined wares on several floors. Green areas with flowers and plants and the never-failing cafés with their tables and umbrellas offer the tourist as well as the native the chance to take a welcome break.

Outside, the hallmark of this shopping center is a tall skyscraper to which broad flights of stairs lead through the gardens.

KIKAR HAMEDINA

This spacious round plaza is in the northeastern part of the city, not far from the North Station. A point of convergence for the important streets and thoroughfares, it is surrounded by numerous elegant shops.

Tel Aviv, the modern skyscraper which houses the City Hall shopping center and two views of the interior with shops and fashionable rendezvous.

Tel Aviv, partial view of the Kikar Hamedina and its shops.

Tel Aviv, pictures showing two aspects of the Israeli
National Museum (Ha'aretz Museum).

HA'ARETZ MUSEUM

The Israeli National Museum or Ha'aretz Museum,
also known as the "Museum of the Land of Israel"
can be considered one of the outstanding museum
complexes in Tel Aviv. Located near the satellite
city of Ramat Aviv, on the other side of the Yarkon
River, it is next to Tel Quasile the archaeological
site which has furnished interesting evidence dating
to various periods. The Museum offers a significant
cross section of the archaeology, history and anthro-
pology of this region.
The museum was conceived and realized in the
1950s and its present eleven pavilions make it possible to choose the area one wishes to see. These
include the *Department of the History of Writing*
(Alphabet); the *Department of Ceramics*, with finds
that range from the Ancient East to the New World;
the *Nehoustan Section*, with finds from the copper
mines of King Solomon in Timna; the *Department
of Glass*, from the Bronze age to the 18th century;
the *Kadman Section* or *Numismatic Museum*; the
department called *Man and his Work*; the
Department of Ethnology and Folklore; of *Science
and Technology* and an interesting *Planetarium*.

Tel Aviv, aerial view of the University and one of the building which houses the faculties.

Beth Hatefutsoth, Museum of the Jewish Diaspora: Jewish portraits from the four corners of the world.

UNIVERSITY

A city which vaunts great cultural traditions, Tel Aviv has a university which is in the vanguard in research in the fields of science, medicine and the various technologies.

The university campus is situated to the north of the city in the suburb of Ramat Aviv. Founded in the latter half of the 1950s, it is now composed of a large number of modern functional buildings which house the various faculties. Traditional Israeli efficiency does not in the least impair its comfort and beauty, for teaching activities, study and research take place in excellently equipped buildings set in the midst of green parks and flowerbeds, abounding in decorative palms.

In addition to the traditional university courses, others are offered dedicated to ecology, the reclamation of desert areas, sources of energy, the development of the Third World, the Middle East and Africa in general, clinical research, diagnostics and communication.

DIASPORA MUSEUM
(Beth Hatefutsoth)

The Beth Hatefutsoth Museum or Nahum Museum of the Jewish Diaspora is, without doubt, one of the best known cultural and tourist centers of Israel.

The Beth Hatefutsoth was never meant to be a sanctuary of the past. It presents the history of the 2,500 years of the Jewish Diaspora as a vital and stimulating experience. Over four million visitors of all ages, Jews and non-Jews, Israelis and tourists, have crossed its threshold since its inauguration in 1978. While the principal purpose of most museums is that of collecting, preserving and exhibiting authentic objects of great historical and artistic value, that of the Diaspora Museum, in view of the unusual nature of the material, is to invent completely different exhibition criteria capable of showing, contemporaneously, the development of the Jewish communities in the various countries and situations. Instead of presenting a chronology of Jewish histo-

41

Beth Hatefutsoth, Museum of the Jewish Diaspora: Titus Arch - Replica; enlarged from Titus Arch in Rome.

Beth Hatefutsoth, Museum of the Jewish Diaspora: Circumcision ceremony, North Africa, 19ᵗʰ century. Sculpture group.Africa, XIX sec.

ry, the Permanent Exhibition is articulated around six basic themes of Jewish survival. Family life, the community, the religion, culture, the relationship with the non-Jewish world, and the return to Zion are presented using high-tech equipment such as computers, audio-visual aids, multi-vision screens, three-dimensional representations and models. Another feature of the Museum are the consultation areas, to be found on each floor, where the visitor can see films of his choice and research data on the more than three thousand Jewish communities and on the meaning of the over ten thousand Jewish names.

Even more interesting is the Dorot Israelite Geneological Center, the

*Beth Hatefutsoth, Museum of the Jewish Diaspora:
Jewish wedding in Galicia in 19ᵗʰ century with the musicians
(kleyzmerim) in background.*

Beth Hatefutsoth, Museum of the Jewish Diaspora:
Painted ceiling of the wooden Synagogue in Chodorow,
near Lvov. Built in 1632; painting dated 1914. Replica.

Beth Hatefutsoth, Museum of the Jewish Diaspora: Ecclesia and Synagoga.
Original statues in Strasbourg Cathedral, 1230. Replica.

first of its kind in the world, a computerized archive of the Jewish
geneologies of the entire world, where the families can preserve their
histories for future generations and unite them with other families.
The Beth Hatefutsoth is not a memorial, a monument to the memory.
Its purpose is that of opening new perspectives to Hebraism, of supply-
ing new ways of understanding it. The Museum represents the future.
As one of its founders, the poet Abba Kovner, said "... a nation which
lives solely attached to its past is dead, but if the Jews can derive
awareness and love from their patrimony, they will have the force to
open the doors to the future."

Beth Hatefutsoth, Museum of the Jewish Diaspora:
"One Culture many Facets". Wall painting by Dan Kerman.

Tel Aviv, views of the modern trade center of the Diamond Exchange; bottom: aerial view of the Ayalon Freeway.

Tel Aviv, a view of the futuristic ensemble of monumental elements which decorate Edith Wolfson Park.

DIAMOND EXCHANGE

The modern commercial center of the Diamond Exchange stands out against the sky with its unmistakeable skyscrapers, in the suburban agglomerate of Ramat Gan, in the northeastern portion of the large city. A city in itself, Ramat Gan was developed by a settlement of Canadian Jews.

EDITH WOLFSON PARK

Despite the exceptional proliferation of the urban fabric, Tel Aviv is a metropolis full of parks and green spaces. Of particular note among the city's various 'lungs' is this park with a unique futuristic monument in line with the modern aspect of the city.

BIRD SAFARI

There are any number of things the tourist can do in this surprising city. One of them is to go on a real safari in the midst of tropical birds.

The varicolored exotic avifauna live in freedom, in a kind of specially equipped zoo where the faithfully reconstructed natural environments favor the acclimatization of the numerous species.

In addition to observing and photographing these charming feathered friends from up close, performances are organized which amuse and enchant both large and small.

Tel Aviv, exotic parrots at Bird Safari and an open-air spectacle.

Tel Aviv, aerial view of the Marina.

THE CITY ON THE SEA

To speak of Tel Aviv today as it is, a modern, scintillating, functional and vanguard city, also means stressing the fact that this Middle Eastern metropolis is first and foremost one of the most qualified, well-equipped, and therefore popular resorts for residential and seaside tourism.

The town began on the sea and developed there, projected seawards. Tel Aviv has a tourist, seaside and recreational dimension not to be taken lightly, when one takes into account, just for an instant, that what we have here is the most seducing fashionable locality, frequented and appreciated by tourists and Israeli vacationers in the first place, but also by those who come from abroad. Tel Aviv is after all the city where you go to have fun and live a high life. The youth of Tel Aviv, and of the country in general, come here to enjoy themselves in the various gathering places and fashionable rendezvous.

For kilometers and kilometers, the broad beach with its fine sand slopes towards the transparent and safe sea shoals. The beaches of Tel Aviv, almost all public with the exception of those parts reserved for the hotels, are particularly suitable for family vacations with small children. The sandy shores continue uninterruptedly, from the mouth of the Yarkon, to the north, up to the city of Jaffa, on the south. The broad promenades are lined with palm-shaded sidewalks with a never-ending flow of residents and tourists who promenade back and forth while cafés with bands, lights, sounds and orchestras make the evenings come alive. The large hotel and residential complexes, including some of the most prestigious and qualified names in high-class international accommodation facilities, run along the seaside promenade, *Herbert Samuel Street*, and *Hayarkon Street*. Restaurants, pizza parlors, fashionable cafés and various gathering places assure the best in food and entertainment.

47

Tel Aviv. These pictures give us an idea of the tourist port, the hotels and the rendezvous which characterize the city's promenade.

The tourist port (*Marina*) offers shelter and moorage to a large number of pleasure crafts, as well as the facilities required for windsurfing, sailing and nautical sports in general. A swimming pool, with a constant year-round temperature, and a Dolphinarium (enclosure for spectacles with dolphins) complete the panorama of the seaside attractions of Tel Aviv.

Tel Aviv, enticing views of the city, in the part
overlooking the litoral, with modern hotels, seaside
boulevards and walks, rendezvous and recreational
infrastructures. Above: the Hotel Hilton.

Tel Aviv, two views of the typical
modern buildings overlooking the
promenade. In the foreground: the
Hotel Dan with the facade painted
by Yaacov Agam.

Tel Aviv, flowerbeds, but above all
palms, characterize the lovely
promenade.

Tel Aviv, looking towards the
beach, with the modern pavilions
which house the cafés and invite
the visitor to take a break.

Tel Aviv. Following pages: the
spacious bathing beach, a view of
the skyscrapers facing the
promenade and a detail of the
latter.

Jaffa, panorama from Tel Aviv with the original
nucleus stretching out towards the sea.

Jaffa, the Clock Tower.

Jaffa, two characteristic corners of the original
nucleus of the city.

YAFFO

You can't say you have seen Tel Aviv unless you've
also seen Jaffa, which by now is a single conurba-
tion with the great Israeli metropolis. The best time
to go is in the evening or at night, when the artists'
quarter, the fashionable nightspots and characteristic
meeting places take on life, filled with a cosmopoli-
tan and varied crowd, all out for a good time.
Unlike Tel Aviv, historically so new and, as we
have seen, a direct offshoot of Jaffa, the latter has a
millenary history whose roots go back to biblical
times, often mixing myth with actual history.
Already mentioned as *Yapou* in an Egyptian source
of the sixteenth century B.C., the city has ancient
Phoenician origins. Pliny attributes its foundation to
Joppa, daughter of Aliolos, about 4000 years before
Christ. According to Hebrew tradition, it was
Japheth, one of Noah's sons, who founded it on a
hill, shortly after having left the mythical ark, which
had come to rest on Mount Ararat after the Flood. In
the tradition of the Old Testament we find *Yafo*, 'the

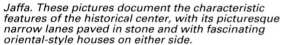

Jaffa. These pictures document the characteristic features of the historical center, with its picturesque narrow lanes paved in stone and with fascinating oriental-style houses on either side.

Jaffa, the church of St. Peter and a detail of the bell tower.

Jaffa, the bell tower of St. Peter dominates this typical meeting place.

beautiful'; known as *Joppe* by the Greeks, it was called *Joppa* by the Romans and *Yafa* by the Arabs. Its ideal position made it a prosperous trading center, from antiquity on, with a busy harbor. At the time of the Judaic War, the city was taken and its population exterminated (66 A.D.); two years later it was razed to the ground by Vespasian. From the Crusades on, the history of Jaffa is a constant turnover of peoples, conquests, destruction and reconstruction. Napoleon, his army decimated by a serious form of the plague, was there in 1799 and it then passed to the Egyptians and the Turks. Jewish immigration to Jaffa dates from the 1920s. Afterwards, the accentuation of the phenomenon led to the creation of a Jewish colony which amalgamated with the pre-existing Arab community. At the end of World War I the city passed under British control, and was then annexed by the new state of Israel (1948). In 1950 the administration of Jaffa and Tel Aviv were fused into one. Destruction and

subsequent reconstruction was a pattern in its millenary history, and this means that the vestiges of Jaffa's earliest times are rather few. The last reconstruction and urban renewal dates to the early 1960s. The harbor itself, once so flourishing, is now almost exclusively a fishing port.

Among the better-known features of this city, which has preserved a Levantine character in its oldest portion, mention should be made of the **Clock Tower** (1906), the 17th-century **Church of St. Peter**, which stands on the site of a Crusader fortress and a Franciscan monastery, the **Great Mosque** (*Mahmudiye Mosque*, 1812), the picturesque **artists' quarter**, the **Archaeological Museum**, with evidence and documentation of the city's history and its urban development.

Jaffa, two views of the fishing port.

Jaffa, the lighthouse seen from the wharves of the port.

Jaffa, view of the houses overlooking the harbor basin.

Jaffa, fascinating panorama of Tel Aviv and its skyscrapers.

Jaffa, the War Memorial dominates the panoramic lookout over Tel Aviv.

Jaffa, fishing boats anchored in the port.

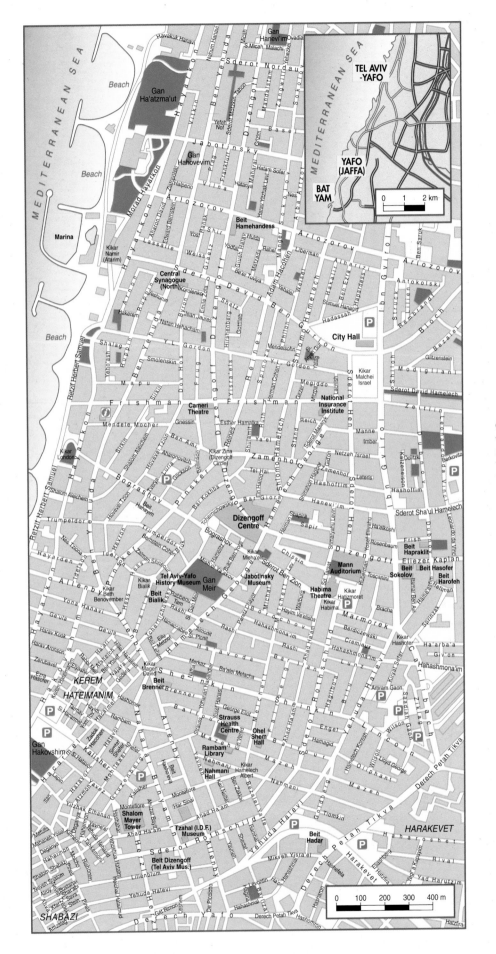

© Copyright 1994 by
Casa Editrice Bonechi
via Cairoli 18/b
50131 Firenze - Italia
Tel. 55/576841 - Fax 55/5000766
Telex 571323 CEB -

Printed in Italy by Centro Stampa Editoriale Bonechi.

Text: Giuliano Valdes - Editing Studio, Pisa.

Translation: Erika Pauli.

Photographs from the Archives of Casa Editrice Bonechi taken by Paolo Giambone. Aerial photographs on pages 2, 40 top, 44 bottom and 47, were kindly provided by Albatross Aerial Photography, Tel Aviv.

The Publishers thank the Tel Aviv Museum of Art, the Museum of the Jewish Diaspora and the Rubin Museum for their kind cooperation.

ISBN 88-8029-172-6

★ ★ ★